What to see in
Grassington, Linton and Threshfield

by

Elizabeth Raistrick

D1827448

Linton packhorse bridge

Dalesman Books
1971

20p

The Dalesman Publishing Company Ltd.,
Clapham (via Lancaster), Yorkshire

First Publised 1971

© Elizabeth Raistrick 1971

Front cover by Celia King

1SBN: 0 85206 114 5

Galava Printing Company Limited
Hallam Road, Nelson, Lancashire

Grassington, Linton & Threshfield

Introduction

GRASSINGTON is one of the best-known villages in the North-West Yorkshire Dales, a favourite calling place for coaches, motorists and other tourists. It is easily accessible from the industrial areas of the West Riding and the North-East of Lancashire, being near enough for an afternoon's run or even a summer evening's visit. It has far more shops, hotels and cafes than any neighbouring village, so that visitors often stay for an hour or two. But so often they walk rather aimlessly round the place, not quite sure what to look at, or even what is worth looking at. Yet it is in many ways a typical "Dales" village, and its features of interest, once known, can be recognised in many other villages. This booklet is an attempt to show what to look for, and how to recognise features of architectural and historic interest. Walks round each village are planned as well as a walk to the church and from one village to another with longer and shorter variations. None is beyond the capacity of quite ordinary walkers of all ages.

Grassington, Linton, Threshfield and Hebden together form the ecclesiastical parish of Linton, though each village (or township) is a separate civil parish, appointing a representative to the Skipton Rural District Council. The church is not in the heart of any one of these villages, but is down on the riverside in a position roughly central to all of them, and connected by age-old footpaths to each village.

Who built these villages and when were they built?

THIS is the question most frequently asked by visitors, either students collecting materials for a "thesis," schoolchildren making a "study of a village" while on a school journey, casual trippers or tourists. It is quite impossible to answer this question, but it is perhaps not an unreasonable one for young people to ask who are familiar with "housing estates" built all at one time by a local authority or a development company. They cannot imagine a village growing naturally by stages over a long period of time as the population increased, and the replacement of older primitive dwellings by newer improved ones, by decay and re-building, or even by change of user as old houses become relegated to barns, out-houses and sheds. Today, we even see the reversal of this process as well-built old barns are converted into dwelling-houses!

The names of this group of villages Grassington, Linton, Threshfield—are typical Anglian names, given by the people who came to this country to settle during the period of the fourth to the seventh centuries A.D. They came from the continent of Europe, entering by the east coast and working up the estuaries, river valleys and other easy routes. As our villages are far over to the west of England, it was inevitably in the later times that the Anglian settlers reached here, and so came not as conquerors but as peaceful settlers. The early settlements were probably made by fairly large groups follow-ing a definite leader. Their new villages were then named after the leader, so emphasising the group character—for example "Bolling" meant the "settlement made by the people of Bolla." Later, smaller groups, possibly only single families, pushed further up into the Dales as true pioneers venturing into unknown and possibly almost uninhabited areas. The Angles must have met some of the earlier British people, as they took over the old names for some, at least, of the physical features. This is particularly true of river names; Ouse, Wharfe, Aire, Calder are all pre-Anglian names, and so is Pen-y-ghent.

The later village names were less personal and usually related to natural features or to the use of the land. So Grassington *may* mean the "grazing or pasture land," though it may be derived equally well from a personal name, "Gars." There are still in Grassington a Garrs Lane and a Garrs End, while Grass Wood is referred to in mediaeval documents as Silva Garrs. Grassington occupies the most favoured site for an early settlement, as it lies on a fairly level shelf above the first sharp rise from the river, it faces south-west and is protected from the north by the rising land behind it. As long as records exist, it has always been the largest of the villages. It had two small streams, now culverted for most of their journey to the river, and a powerful spring in the lowest south-east corner (opposite to the church on the other bank). The remnant of primitive woodland still existing in Bastow Wood, suggests that the woods were of an open character with scattered trees and shrubs and varied herbaceous undergrowth. This could be easily cleared to make small pastures which could be gradually enlarged as more land was needed for cultivation and pasture as the population increased.

Linton, which means "the flax enclosure," and Threshfield, which means the "threshing field," probably arose as outlying small hamlets when Grassington expanded. Later they each grew into independent villages with their own cultivated fields. By the time of Domesday Book (1086) they were all three separate, with their own overlords. Linton stands on a belt of low morainic hills—stony debris left along the sides of the main valley as the Wharfedale glacier retreated at the end of the Ice Age. This debris dammed the small stream that we know as Linton Beck, forming a shallow lake that spread southwards for a mile or two towards Cracoe. This lake persisted as a small tarn and marsh until it was finally drained about 1850. The marshy land was continually re-fertilised by every flood and so was ideal for growing flax (lin), which was one of the essential raw materials for clothes. Even as late as 1812, Whitaker in his *History of Craven* speaks of the flax-growing round Linton and the "retting" or rotting of the plant in great stone troughs down by the beckside in the village. The morainic gravels gave good, dry and well-drained sites for building in Linton, well above any floods. They also gave firm footing in the stream bed so that Linton had several easy fords where the beck could be crossed.

Threshfield also stands where its local beck cuts through the same moraine. Here, as at Linton, the gravel of the moraine gave firm footing for crossing the beck, so Threshfield also had a ford long before it had a bridge. It also stands well above flood level. In fact, one notices that all the older parts of the Dales villages are built in tributary valleys with small streams, not on the main river, and so are safely above the floods.

The first written records of these villages occur in the Domesday Book (1187), and are very short and scanty. The Dales were remote areas, difficult of access, so the officers of William I did not themselves go into them, to collect information. Instead, the headman of each village had to journey to

York to give evidence of ownership before and after the Conquest, and of taxable value. We can imagine the problems of a Norman French clerk taking evidence from Anglian peasants whose dialect was mainly Anglian, but with many Norse words and Norse alterations to words, and then recording that evidence in Latin! No wonder it is scanty! There is no mention of mill or of church, though we know there were pre-Conquest churches (perhaps only of wood) at Burnsall, Kirkby Malham and Gargrave. The Domesday Book does not give any actual numbers of people living in each village, but by comparison with other records we can suggest very approximately what was the size of each village. Later, in 1285, an inquiry known as Kirby's Inquest gives more information as to the area of land cultivated in each village, and hence by inference, as each was self-supporting, an idea of the population. The Poll Tax of 1379 gives the name of every man (with his wife) who paid tax, and also every unmarried person of more than 16 years of age. So we know the number of families in each village and can estimate the probable total of population. Putting these records together, we get the following table which suggests small villages growing very slowly, completely self-contained, and agriculturally speaking in a relatively poverty-stricken area.

Probable number of families living in each village

	Domesday Book 1087	Kirby's Inquest 1285	Poll Tax 1379
Grassington	12	24	26
Linton	8	16?	11
Threshfield	8	12	18
Hebden (includes Thorpe)	12	12	14

Some time in the twelfth century, a church was built in Linton. The question invariably asked is "Why was it built where it is, down on the river bank, and not in any one village?" Again, no one can give an answer; one can only make conjectures. This church has always served all four villages. Four "church paths" converge on it even today, though some have become incorporated in modern roads and others have been diverted a little at the time of the Enclosures (1792). It is in fact very central to all the villages, and was almost equidistant at a time when people were used to walking as a matter of course. Who built this church, and why from the earliest records until 1866 were there two rectories in Linton parish? Again we do not *know*, but we can suggest that two local landowners gave land for its endowment (glebe land) as well as tithes of all produce, and that in consequence each donor was entitled to nominate an incumbent. A tablet in the church gives the names of all the rectors of the two medieties (the two halves of the parish) from 1229 until 1866 when the two were united.

For much of the history of the parish, the four townships belonged to quite different lords of the manor. They passed by the marriages of heiresses or sometimes by purchase into a variety of families. Not until quite late did most of the land come into the hands of the Clifford family and so to the Dukes of Devonshire. But even they have never held Hebden township. Linton and Threshfield from the fourteenth century were held by the Radcliffes of Threshfield, and from them passed on by the marriage of an heiress to the lords of Rylstone, Cracoe and Hetton. Again by the marriage of an heiress, all these passed into the hands of the Nortons of Norton Conyers in the fifteenth century. After the Rising of the North (1569), the Norton lands were confiscated, and after being for some years in the hands of the Crown passed to the Earls of Cumberland (the Cliffords of Skipton Castle). The Cliffords acquired half of Grassington by inheritance from yet another heiress and the other half by purchase. But Hebden had quite a different history. It was for many years held by the Tempests of Bracewell and Bolling, who in 1568 sold the Lordship to the free-holders of Hebden. Thus today any income from the remaining manorial rights, such as mineral and water royalties, is divided among the freeholders according to the ancient rents of their predecessors.

Grassington has always been the largest village, at least since any records were kept. Two very old roads met here. One ran from Fountains Abbey to Malham Moor, where the abbey had lands, and continued even as far as the Lake District. A stretch of this old road became a part of the Skipton–Pateley Bridge–Ripon turnpike and is still well used as the B6265. Other parts, such as that from Grassington over Malham Moor and beyond, are today represented by green roads and foot-paths. Another road came from Skipton and the south and continued northward to Wensleydale (B6166), later becoming part of the Otley–Leyburn turnpike. Hence the ford and later the bridge at Grassington have always been important. This village had a weekly market and an annual fair until the middle of the nineteenth century, and these brought traders and goods from outside the area. The development of lead mining on Grassington Moor after the middle of the eighteenth century brought miners from Alston Moor, Weardale, Swale-dale, Derbyshire and even from Cornwall! When the local watermills were no longer needed for grinding grain, as it could be bought easily in Skipton, they were adapted into small textile mills largely for spinning woollen yarn. The smaller mills up-dale in villages like Arncliffe and Kettlewell could not be used for weaving, which became concentrated on both sides of the Wharfe at Linton and Grassington. This brought workers from the upper villages and even from adjacent parts of Wensleydale as well as from parts of Airedale and places as far down the Wharfe as Addingham. Thus by 1851 Grassington had a population of 1,138 of very varied birthplaces. The closing-down of the mines and later of the textile mills led to a gradual decline in population to 494 in 1901.

The opening of the Dales Railway in 1901 reversed this movement until in 1961 the population had reached the level of 1851. The increased accessibility brought visitors and led to the opening of boarding houses and more shops. People working in Skipton or even in Bradford found they could live in Grassington or Threshfield. Retired people bought up old cottages or built new ones and the quarrying industry developed rapidly and so provided more work. Threshfield, Linton and Hebden also benefited by the railway but to a less extent. Wartime brought temporary increases in 1914–21, and again in 1939–51, but these declined after the wars. Increased population led to a demand for better facilities for the supply of water and electricity and for drainage. So the water supplies were im-proved and extended; the electricity supply, starting as a small hydro-electric scheme, expanded until it was taken over by the nationalised electricity industry; and mains drainage was connected to all but the most outlying houses. This in turn has led to the rural district council building a large housing estate in Grassington and a smaller one in Threshfield. Private building has also developed to a considerable extent because of the presence of these amenities.

Today, Grassington is the most important and the largest village in Upper Wharfedale. It has more shops, more inns and restaurants, more new housing, and together with Linton and Threshfield, more places of worship, more schools and more industry than any other centre in the dale.

Grassington remembers only two of her former citizens, judging from the various books that are written about the village. These two are Tom Lee, who murdered a local Dr. Petty because of a fancied insult, and Thomas Airey who was so stage-struck after seeing a theatrical performance that he formed a company of local men and opened a small theatre in an old barn at the top of Garrs End Lane. But Linton and Threshfield remember their two great benefactors—Matthew Hewitt who endowed the Free Grammar School, and Richard Fountaine who founded the Almshouses in Linton. These two villages also produced their martyrs, who joined the Rising in the North as a protest against the rack-renting of the London merchants and others who had bought the confiscated monastic estates after the dissolution of the monasteries. The Rising failed, and the ordinary peasants were harshly punished and sent back to their own villages to be executed there by fellow villagers, so as to show what happened to rebels. We know the names of the local ones—Robert Arraye, William Whiteacre, alias Stable, Thomas Styrke, all of Threshfield, and Nicholas Hewitt and Edward Wilkinson of Linton.

A Walk Round Grassington

THE tithe map of 1841 shows the plan of Grassington as a rather elongated Y with a cross line above it. The Y runs a little east of north to west of south, while the cross line extends roughly north-west to south-east and can be traced as a footpath behind the council houses as far as the last houses to the east. It crosses the main road and continues down to the river, past the Low Mill, and by a long-disused ford links up with an old path on the hillside, finally reaching Skipton. In

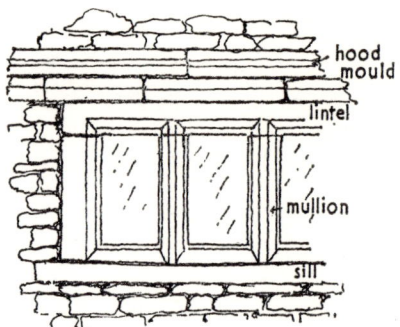

Types of windows. From left to right: Mullioned window, c. 1630; Georgian sash window; Mullion and transom, late 17th century. (Fig. 3).

1841 building was fairly continuous along these old Grassington roads in the form of cottages, workshops and shops. By 1891 the Ordnance Survey maps show that the gaps had been filled in almost completely—the result of the increased population when miners and textile workers moved into the village. This close built-up area is the only interesting part of Grassington, for all the rest of the buildings are of post-1900 date.

As most cars park in or near the Square, it is most convenient to make this the starting point. The lowest part of the Square is known as Town End, and the houses here have all been much altered. At the corner, where the bank now stands, there was formerly an inn—the *Jobbers' Arms*. Next to it is an old smithy used as such right up to the last few years. On the opposite side the confectioner's shop is a nineteenth century building, while the Co-operative Stores are on the site of the stables for the old horse buses and charabancs of the pre-1914 war era. On the right hand side is a typical "fold," Pletts Fold (Fig. 1–1), characteristic of the planning of Grassington. The folds were *not* built as a defence against the Scots, though that is an explanation often suggested. Most old towns have very similar features though with different names—in Skipton they are called yards. They represent an early small "croft," attached to a particular house, and then gradually infilled with newer cottages as the village or town grew. In early days, people really liked to live very close to their neighbours, who had in the first place chosen the original site because of nearness to water or shelter from winds or some other good reas on. The

folds housed a small compact community. In Pletts Fold, one cottage has an old dated doorhead, "H.E.A. 1744," with one good mullioned window in an upper storey. At the end of the fold a "Georgian" house has a good doorway.

Returning to the Square, we notice two outstanding houses. The one on the west of the road is Church House (Fig. 1–F), with many seventeenth century features. There is a continuous drip moulding above the ground floor windows which are all mullioned. On the floor above is an inserted Georgian sash window, and above the door a datestone with the initials "S.A.P. 1694." From this we can deduce, with the help of the Parish Registers, that it was built for Stephen and Alice Peart. The house, with its thick walls and heavy stone-slated roof, is an excellent example of a yeoman's house—three rooms wide but only one room deep (apart from a modern extension at the north end). This is a type of house seen in many of the Dales villages, often with alterations to windows yet still recognisable from its plan and its structure. These houses were often built by prosperous yeomen farmers who had gradually improved their position in the hundred years or more after the dissolution of the monasteries. They quite naturally invested some of their increased wealth in the building of a substantial house, larger and more comfortable than their old ones, and embodying on the headstone above the main door the date of building and the initials of the owner and often his wife also.

On the opposite side of the Square is Grassington House (Fig. 1–A), just as typical of the late eighteenth century, with its high sash windows with numerous small panes of glass, its central doorway, and the symmetrical placing of the windows on each floor. It was built by a Mr. Brown, one of the promoters of the Grassington–Pateley Bridge turnpike, but soon passed into the hands of one of the Allcock family, who in the late eighteenth century were bankers (the original Craven Bank) and interested in promoting turnpike roads, canals, mining ventures and other enterprises. This family also built Newfield Hall at Airton and Aireville at Skipton.

Though there is no other large Georgian house in Grassington, we can see how this building influenced people and led to the modernising and improvement of the older houses in the late eighteenth and early nineteenth centuries. Most of the houses along Main Street and up Garrs End Lane are quite old but their frontages have been altered, though older seventeenth century windows may still remain at the backs of the houses. This is a useful tip when seeking to estimate the earliest date of building. The windows at the back of the house which served kitchen, scullery, pantry or staircase are much less likely to have been altered than the ones at the front which lighted the living rooms and the bedrooms. Another test of age, not quite so definite, is to look at the roofs and chimneys. The seventeenth century builders usually put a heavy stone coping on the roof at the gable ends, ending in a "kneeler" which would often support a gable ornament, such as a stone lantern or a stone globe. They also built good chimneys of dressed stone slabs, not raised much above the level of the ridge of the roof and finished with a neat, well-made cornice. The eighteenth and nineteenth century chimneys are less likely to be ornamented or made into an architectural feature. The owners of old houses throughout the centuries have altered and "improved" their houses, just as modern householders do. Apart from alterations to the windows, the changes most usually made would be to build up the old large "arched" fireplaces and insert more modern ones. Often they removed the old stone staircases and built wooden ones in a more convenient position. But these internal alterations do not show from the outside.

We can leave the Square by the former cobbled road, Main Street, at the top left-hand corner, or by the lane, Garrs Lane, in the right-hand corner. Up Garrs Lane there are no very interesting buildings, though it is always interesting to look out for signs of alterations, until one reaches the top of the lane. Here on the right is the Congregational Church (Fig. 1–B) and its burial ground. Built in 1812 it was the earliest Nonconformist church to be erected in Grassington. Prior to this the members of this church worshipped at the Independent (Congregational) Church in Winterburn, a lovely seventeenth century building. Both Independents and Quakers, early Nonconformist bodies, were very strong in the Dales at one time, especially in the years between the mid-seventeenth century and the end of the eighteenth century. Opposite the Congregational Church is an old building (Fig. 1–C), originally a barn as the stone arch of the old entry shows, but now converted to cottages. This was at one time used as a theatre by Tom Airey, who has been said by one writer to be a bumpkin but who must have had some ability as actor and manager as he persuaded Edmund Keane and Harriet Mallon to appear in some of his productions.

The street across the top of Garrs Lane is Scar Street, dwindling into a footpath and ultimately reaching the river. Turning to the left along this street we come to a large old stone barn (Fig. 1–D), known locally as Wesley Barn as John Wesley is reputed to have preached in it. Whether he did or not, the barn is worth some attention. At one side of the entry porch are well-made arched slits in the wall to ensure ventilation, while at the other side is a pigeon cote. Inside this are the old nesting

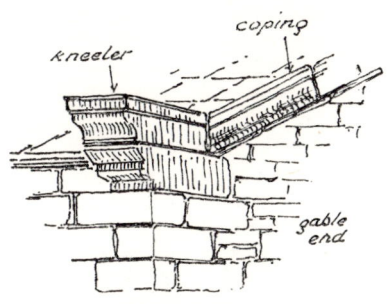

Roof details. (Fig. 4).

boxes built in the wall—the lower part was cut off by a floor and used as a stone dog kennel. The doorway itself has the broken remnants of an old pegged oak door, and on the door head is the date 1683. As we approach the head of Main Street we pass the backs of cottages known as Well Head—or are they really the fronts with the backs into Main Street?

The route now is by Chapel Street, Garrs End Lane and the Woggins. On our right hand at the head of the Main Street is the Devonshire Institute, often called the Town Hall (Fig. 1–E). This building is used for a variety of purposes—political meetings, parish council meetings, exhibitions, concerts and dramatic performances. At one time, cinema shows at the weekend attracted people from up and down the dale as well as local residents. Across from us, slightly left, is Chamber End Fold or King Street (Fig. 1–8). The first house is an interesting seventeenth century one, although inevitably it shows signs of alterations in the eighteenth and nineteenth centuries. The attic storey has a good three-light window with mullions. The smaller houses at the lower end of this "Fold" were built for the lead miners in the early nineteenth century; they normally had a "minimum" house with two rooms up and two rooms down. Most have been modernised and in some cases two cottages made into one.

Proceeding along Chapel Street, a date stone "1851" comes from a period when Grassington was expanding. Many of the houses along this street belong to this era. On the left is another "fold," Chapel Fold, with the old Primitive Methodist chapel (1837) now converted into a workshop where fine-quality furniture is made. This was sometimes called "Ranters' Fold" (Fig. 1–7) from the nickname given to the early Primitive Methodists. Next is a block of new flats across the entry to Pattinson Fold, where there is a very good old house. Its roof has cornices finished with "kneelers" at the gable end, and the chimneys also have neat cornices. Further along on the right hand side of Chapel Street is a corner house, "Grasmere" (1896), standing at the entry to another fold, Hill Top Fold. The oldest building is at the top of the fold, with a good doorway. Still further along is Sam Hill, more properly called Intake Lane, rising steeply and paved. Some of the houses in this corner have very good regularly coursed stone work with "quarry pointing," sloped so as to shed the rain down the wall and not into it.

We continue with buildings of various types—an old barn with traces of old windows, miners' cottages and additions and extensions—a typical mixture covering the history of three centuries. Another old road, Bank Lane, leads up into the fields. At the end of Chapel Street is a group of early buildings. The one called Inglenook, dated 1628, has been partly rebuilt but retains some of its early features such as a "string" course between the lower and upper storeys and old "drip" mouldings over the windows, although the space between the mullions has been increased to allow the insertion of wider windows. The upper windows still retain the narrow lights. It is easy to see where an extension has been built on to an older building, as the quoins (the large corner stones) of the original wall are very clear and obvious.

The last house along here is Town Head Farm, which belongs to the Trustees of the Fountaine Hospital in Linton and farms most of the land from here towards Conistone. It has many interesting features, including a two-storied porch with hood moulding to the window and string course below it. The window is spoiled by the eaves-spouting being carried across it. In the main part of the house, the upper windows are three-light mullioned, and the lower ones four-light, all with drip stones above them. Below the roof line is an unusual ornamental border built-up from pebbles in semi-circles. The left hand part of the building was formerly an out-house, but has had the lower storey made into living space. The old barn belonging to the farm has pigeon holes under the eaves.

We now turn left and pass Scaw Ghyll, on the site of and partly incorporating the Old (Manorial) Mill, based on a small stream which has now gone underground. On the right we pass Cove Lane leading towards Grass Wood, with Bull Ing Lane straight ahead and Garrs End Lane to the left, up which we turn until we reach Moody Stye Lane leading down to Wood Lane. We continue ahead past the lower end of Chamber End Fold into a narrow lane which becomes a very narrow "ginnel" emerging at last into Main Street by a passage *under* the chemist's shop. This is a very old right-of-way, older than the buildings which hem it in. We can now continue down the

Main Street. Across the street is a group of "Georgian" houses
with typical doorways and staircase window. This is Armstrong
Hill, or more commonly "Neddy Hill" (Fig. 1–5). Down the
Street the houses and shops have been altered beyond recog-
nition, though the backs of the buildings show earlier features.
The fruit shop is labelled "Tom Lee's Smithy," Tom Lee being
the murderer who is commemorated by most writers about
Grassington. Passing down and looking at the various houses
set back from the street, we see Ashfield House (Fig. 1–11), a
pleasant late seventeenth or more likely early eighteenth
century building with squared mullions to the windows. Then
after more "improved" cottages, we pass Jacobs Fold (Fig.
1–12) and below that an old footpath, not labelled but known
as "Jakey." It runs at the foot of the gardens of the houses that
face into the Square, and on the outside of the grounds of the
Old Hall. This is one of the oldest inhabited houses in the dale
but has been much altered over the centuries. The windows that
are usually called fourteenth century (on the east wall) may be
later insertions but we cannot be certain. Jakey probably got
its name because it was the narrow lane leading past the Jakes
(back houses, privies, toilets—whatever you like to call them)
at a time when there were no "inside toilets" and no "water-
carried sewage." The "night-soil" man could reach these
"necessary conveniences" without going into the gardens!

This brings us into the main road (Wood Lane) close to the
foot of the Square, to which we return after passing the
tempting windows of the Gallery. In this way we have seen
almost all of the old Grassington. The rest of Grassington —
the houses along Hebden Road, Station Road, Wood Lane and
Moody Stye Lane—are all twentieth century and of no great
interest.

Grassington to Linton, Linton Church and Threshfield

THE visitor to Grassington may want to venture a little
further and see the nearby villages, and anything of interest
on the way. The motorist can take his car directly across the
stone bridge and turn sharp left to pass a number of old
buildings and houses. In fact, until Linton Mill is reached,
there are no entirely new buildings. This road is one way of

getting to the church, which can also be reached by a footpath through the fields. For the walk, we turn down through a stile immediately before the bridge on the left of the road, and this takes us quite definitely *down* to the riverside. It is worth while to spare a few minutes to walk *under* the bridge and note a number of features. The bridge has obviously been widened at some time, and the curvature of the new part is not identical with the curvature of the older, downstream half; this part also shows "mason marks." Looking again at the bridge from the footpath, we can see that the original "humpback" was lifted, by infilling with masonry, at the Grassington end to give an even rise to Station Road. Later a parapet was put on the bridge. This is quite typical—the early bridges had no parapets and were very dangerous on dark nights! The lifting of the roadway accounts for the marked drop from the road to the fields, both upstream and downstream, on the Grassington side of the bridge. There is no corresponding drop on the Threshfield side, but we shall meet an identical case in Linton where the modern road level was lifted when the 1892 bridge was built.

Continuing on the field path, we note a very ugly building on the opposite bank, linked with a dam across the river. This is the site of the original hydro-electric plant of the early part of this century. When the water above the dam is run out to its natural level, the real rocky channel of the Wharfe is clearly seen. We pass by stiles through the fields and emerge at the head of Linton Falls, at the foot of the old path from Grassington locally known as the Flags or the Snake Walk. The barn on the other side of the path has a date stone and good but simple head stones for door and window. We cross the river by the so-called "Tin Bridge," which replaced an earlier structure washed away in a great flood at the turn of the century. That bridge at a still earlier date replaced a simpler wooden crossing. As we follow the path on the Linton bank of the river, winding round the cottages on the left, we see on the right an attractive small stone bridge, probably of the fourteenth century, over Captain or Threshfield Beck, which here forms the boundary between Linton and Threshfield. This bridge is part of the old church path from Threshfield, which came across the Tofts, past the old grammar school and Threshfield Mill, and finally on to what is now the road to the church. We turn along this road passing Linton Mill, a relatively recent structure on the site of several earlier buildings. These used the water from Captain beck, or from the main river. Originally a manorial corn mill, later it was used as a worsted mill by the Birkbecks (who introduced worsted mills to Skipton) and later still as a cotton mill. With the decline of textiles in this area, it became a creamery, was burnt down, rebuilt and in the end used for a rayon-and-cotton weaving shed. Beyond is Botany—a mill hamlet built about 1850 for the accommodation of mill workers. The front row was rebuilt some years ago, and the back row modernised quite recently. The mill was closed in 1959 under a "nationalisation" scheme and has stood empty ever since. The original water supply for all these houses was a very strong spring emerging from the steep bank on the right; it is still preserved and runs strongly in the middle of the car park along this road. There are two houses between Botany and the church—Holme House (now divided), at the foot of a path from Linton; and Kirk Yett, at the church gate. Both are on old sites, and have been partly rebuilt and modernised.

The church has some twelfth century Norman arches, but was largely rebuilt and later extended. At some time, Linton parish seems to have been part of a much larger Burnsall parish, whose church has fragments dating back before the Norman Conquest. Linton has never had a tower, presumably a sign of poverty. It was altered in the fifteenth or sixteenth century with square-headed windows and again altered in the nineteenth century to its present condition. A short history of the church is contained in a pamphlet available in the building.

The alternative way to the church is by a very old and rather narrow road with *no parking facilities* until the free park is reached. But it is worth going this way to see the old buildings. Turning sharply to the left over the main road bridge, and note on the left an attractive old house which is frequently mentioned in deeds under its old name of Bridgend. It must have replaced even older buildings, as the river crossing on the monastic road to Fountains Abbey must always have been important. Before a bridge was built, if the river was in spate and the ford above the present bridge unusable, travellers such as monks, pilgrims and peasants would be compelled to wait until the floods went down. An obvious need, and probably as obviously filled, would be an inn where people could wait and obtain food. So the tradition that there was a hospice here is probably correct. The cottage has very characteristic seventeenth century windows and other details, but its roof is *not* characteristic. The roof-pitch is much steeper than is normal in the old dales cottages, and it is roofed with thin Welsh slates, not the heavy Yorkshire stone-slates. This roof-pitch is just what would be needed for a thatched roof, to shed rain quickly, so it suggests that here is a cottage that retained its traditional thatched roof until well into the nineteenth century. Then the railways would make it possible to buy Welsh slates which could be used on the old timbers, instead of using much heavier timbers at a lower pitch to accommodate the heavy stone slates. This cottage is now renamed "Lady Well Cottage," a name formerly attached to the next building. Between these two is a narrow lane leading to a permanent spring only a little above the river level. In time of flood it is submerged, but it runs strongly even when the river is low. This was the main water supply for all the cottages on this road until the Craven Water Board brought a new main along it. The name "Ladywell" suggests a pre-Reformation use of it as "Our Lady's Well." Permanent springs of pure water were so valuable that they were regarded as miraculous and given distinctive names, usually of female saints, like St. Alkelda's Well at Giggleswick (the Ebbing and Flowing Well). The next cottage beyond the two Lady Wells is a nineteenth century rebuilding on an old site, but a datestone links it with the older cottages.

Beyond this cottage, on the upper side of the road, is one of the loveliest old buildings in Wharfedale—Threshfield Free Grammar School founded in 1674 by the will of Matthew Hewitt, one of the rectors of Linton. Its full story is told in *Village Schools: An Upper Wharfedale History* by Elizabeth Raistrick (Dalesman, 1971). An old right-of-way, coming into the road by the side of the school yard, is part of the church path from Threshfield to the parish church. Here it becomes part of the modern road which winds round a very symmetrical hill, "Greenhaw," passing the old Threshfield Mill and its various buildings and two old cottages. The mill was worked by a small leet taken off from Captain beck; it can be traced

from a point near the small plantation and can be seen just over
the wall. The dam, only a small one, is now filled in and forms
a sunken garden belonging to one of the three cottages that
have been made from the old mill. An interesting document of
1603, relating to a lease of this mill from George, Earl of
Cumberland, states clearly that the miller had to plant three
acorns to replace every oak tree that he cut down, and that he
could keep only a small dog, unless a larger dog had its claws
cut, to prevent his poaching the Earl's deer. The path crossed
the beck by the little stone bridge, re-named Lile Emily's
Bridge by a local author but probably built two hundred years
before she was born. On crossing the beck, we pass into Linton
township (see page 5), and unless we want to continue to the
church we can turn right up Great Bank, over the cross-roads,
past a house built before the first world war and the Anderton
Institute, and down into Linton village itself.

A Walk round Linton

WHETHER you enter Linton from Skipton, by the road
from Grassington and Threshfield or from Burnsall, you
will approach the village along the north side of the green
which is cut into two unequal areas by Linton Beck, a shallow
stream running over a gravel bed. The green was formerly
"Waste of the Manor of Linton" belonging to the Lords of the
Manor of Linton (the Dukes of Devonshire). Linton parish
council bought it about 1930 and made a series of bye-laws
regulating its use. No animals are allowed to graze on the
green, no fires to be lit (except the one for November 5th) and
no camping. The chains and posts were erected in 1935 and
have successfully prevented it being turned into a mere car
park. The annual May Festival—dancing round the maypole
and crowning the May Queen—is held here, and the shallow
beck, the green and the triangular plantation provide safe places
for children to play.

Most of the houses and barns in Linton look on to the green,
and have a variety of features typical of many Dales villages,
particularly in the walling and roofing in stone. They are of
varying ages from early seventeenth century up to recent days
but are mostly very much in keeping with each other. Starting

at the bus-stop on the Skipton road we see to the north of the road Linton Old Hall, a very interesting house with many special features. The building shows much of its history in its structure, especially in its windows. The oldest part is the western end, the left-hand part as you look at it, with its mullioned windows of the seventeenth century. This part is only two storeys high, and it has been altered by the removal of some of the mullions to allow larger windows to be inserted. The eastern end, which is three storeys high, stands forward from the older building and is obviously a later addition. The windows are of two distinct types. The attic window and the one over the porch are of the mullion (vertical) and transom (horizontal) type, characteristic of the later seventeenth century and often used by Sir Christopher Wren, as for example in Emmanuel College, Cambridge (1668) and St. Christopher's College, Cambridge (1674) (see page 11, Fig. 3).

The window over the porch has had the lower part of the mullion removed to allow the insertion of a sash window. The four other windows of this building have the same stone framing as these seventeenth century openings, but have sash windows with the typical small panes of the eighteenth century.

It is noticeable that the upper windows have larger panes but fewer of them than the lower windows. No architect of this period would have designed a frontage with four different types of windows, so we can feel sure that here a late seventeenth century extension to a still earlier building was itself "modernised" some time in the early eighteenth century by the alteration of its windows. It is significant that the altered windows are those that belong to the best bedroom and the drawing-room, while the unaltered window and the partly altered one belong to the much less important rooms—the attic and the small porch bedroom. It seems likely that the owner of this house was influenced by the new style of building shown in the Fountaine Hospital (Almshouses) at the southern end of the village. This was built as the result of a generous bequest in 1721 from Sir Richard Fountaine; the fact that he left a considerable sum of money to his niece, Lydia Atkinson, who was the daughter of the owner of Linton Old Hall may also serve to explain the alteration. The Atkinsons later owned and altered Linton House, which stands back from the road behind

Linton Old Hall. Originally a seventeenth century house, as is shown by one surviving mullioned window, it has a new frontage built on in the eighteenth century. This part is a very typical "Georgian" building with three sash windows each side of a central entrance, and seven sash windows quite symmetrically disposed above on the first floor. The attics have sash windows in the gables. These windows had the typical small Georgian panes up to the beginning of this century when the then tenant replaced them by the present plate-glass single-panes though again some "Georgian" windows survive in the attics. Linton House grounds are well known for their display of snowdrops in the spring.

Leaving the Old Hall and passing along the road in front of the inn, we see a number of cottages of no special architectural interest but fitting into the village scene by reason of their stone walls and stone-slated low pitched roofs. Some still have the small-paned sash windows of any date up to 1850, now being replaced by modern ones. Most of these cottages have been brought up to date by the provision of modern amenities such as hot water, bath-rooms and inside sanitation. Up the lane by the side of the inn is a recently renovated building. Once a cottage, then an outbuilding, it is once again a cottage and very attractive. At the south-west corner of the green, two narrow roads diverge. One, known as Garris Lane, soon passes into the fields, but the last house on it with its gable end to the lane is a very typical "yeoman's house" of the seventeenth century, now divided into two cottages with a modern extension at the far end. Where the two lanes diverge is another of these houses, now much disguised by pebbledash on all the outside walls and by some new windows, but still showing its origin internally in the arrangement of the rooms and the old arched fireplace.

The most striking building in Linton is the one that faces the southern end of the green—the "Fountaine Hospital," an almshouse for "six poor men or women." The word hospital is used here in its original meaning of a "refuge," perhaps for the old, for travellers or for the sick. Richard Fountaine was born in Linton in 1639 or 1640, his mother being a sister of Matthew Hewitt who endowed the Free Grammar School in Threshfield. Theirs was a large family and related by marriage to most of the other local "yeoman" families of the seventeenth century—

Window surrounds at Fountaine Hospital. (Fig. 5).

the Proctors, Atkinsons, Fountaines and so on. Young Richard went to London where he became a member of the Merchants' Guild and later an alderman of the City of London. He traded with many parts of Europe and invested in many overseas enterprises, including the Hudson Bay Company, the East India Company and the South Seas Company. He stayed in London during the time of the Great Plague, and later helped to rebuild London after the Great Fire of 1666, probably by importing timber from the Baltic ports. He was a very wealthy man, a millionaire in terms of today's money. He died in 1721, and left a very long and detailed will. In this he directed his executors to buy land in Linton parish to provide an almshouse for "six poor men or women" and to secure an endowment that would suffice for three main objects. These were first to provide "doles" for the six almspeople and for any of his poor relatives, and also to provide "blue stuff gowns lined with green for the almspersons"; secondly, to pay to apprentice four poor boys each year; and thirdly to pay the rector of Linton to read prayers twice weekly in a chapel to be attached to the alms-houses, and to preach a sermon on Whitsunday. The executors bought very wisely, securing farms in Grassington, Hebden and Threshfield, but curiously enough not in Linton township itself. The later history of the almshouses is too long to relate here, but the individual cottages in the building have been completely modernised within the last ten years. Payments are still made for apprentices, and were made to poor but *very* distant relations up to quite recently.

The hospital building is a very unusual one for a small village. It was designed by Sir John Vanbrugh, the architect of Blenheim, Castle Howard and Seaton Delaval, and his chief assistant, Nicholas Hawksmoor. Some of the details, for example the windows surrounds (Fig. 5), are similar to those at Castle Howard. The architects were very economical in their efforts, adapting for this building a design that had been made for another client who never used it! The chapel runs north and south and has only a "conventional" east end. The founder specified "prayers," not "services," to be held in the chapel, and this suggests that like his uncle, Matthew Hewitt, he belonged to the Puritan group and not to the High Church group in the Church of England. Though friendly to the Nonconformists, he never joined them. Originally there was no altar in the church and the seats were arranged round all the walls, but in the middle of the nineteenth century the seating was altered to pews facing the "east" window and a communion table installed. Only "prayers" were said until 1892, when the then rector obtained a "faculty" from the Archbishop so that Communion Services could be held—as they still are on one Sunday in the month.

On the beckside of the almshouse grounds, there is a door in the boundary wall which gives access to three stone steps down to a "dipping pool"—the original water supply for the almshouses! Today the cottages have hot and cold water indoors, bathrooms, inside sanitation, electric cookers, stainless steel sinks, kitchens with ample cupboards, and all the old woodwork and plaster has been replaced by new! The small enclosure between the hospital and the beck was formerly the "pound" or "pin-fold," where straying animals were "impounded" by the pinder until the owner redeemed them by paying a fine.

From the hospital we cross the beck by the "clapper" bridge, the little footbridge closely adjacent to one of the old fords. This is the simplest and probably the oldest bridge in Linton; it formerly stood at the other end of the village beyond the road bridge where there is now a line of stepping stones. It was moved when the main bridge was built in 1892. The simple piers built of large stones and the long slate slabs that form the footway were easily dismantled, and re-built in their present position. The asphalt covering the flags and the railings are fairly recent additions to make the crossing safer, especially at night. Between the "clapper" bridge and the main road bridge there is a fine 14th century pack horse bridge. It was repaired in the late 17th century by Dame Elizabeth Redmayne and the parapet added. It is easy to see the main early building, the collapsed portion roughly rebuilt, and the 17th century addition.

The eastern bank of the stream is much steeper than the west so we reach the road by a series of steps. At the top, along this eastern side of the beck, there are a number of interesting old "yeoman" houses or cottages. They have been altered, improved, divided, but they still retain their essential character. The stone walls and stone-slabbed roofs are much the same as when first built, but windows may have been altered and many improvements made inside. The one named "Beckside" in a little "fold" or yard with two other cottages is very typical. Obviously it is part of a once larger house, its neighbour. The walling is continuous and of the same type for half of Beckside, but the part nearer the road is an addition. The stonework of this part is much cruder (Fig. 6), the windows are taller than they are wide, and the floors are on a lower level than the other part. It may have been added as a cottage for a labourer or originally as an outhouse. The older (eastern) part is very typical of the seventeenth century yeoman's house, being three rooms long but only one room deep. Originally there were three rooms on each floor, but in the larger half one bedroom has been divided and an additional window inserted—the sash window. Victorian sash windows have also been inserted in the eastern end room, but the other mullion windows still remain with the "string course" running above the groundfloor. The two middle doorways have simple headstones, one with initials and date "A 1642 P" (Fig. 7) showing that the house was built by Anthony Proctor, a member of one of the old families. The other doorway has rather flat triangular spandrels, which are repeated in the wide fireplace of the room inside. The porches

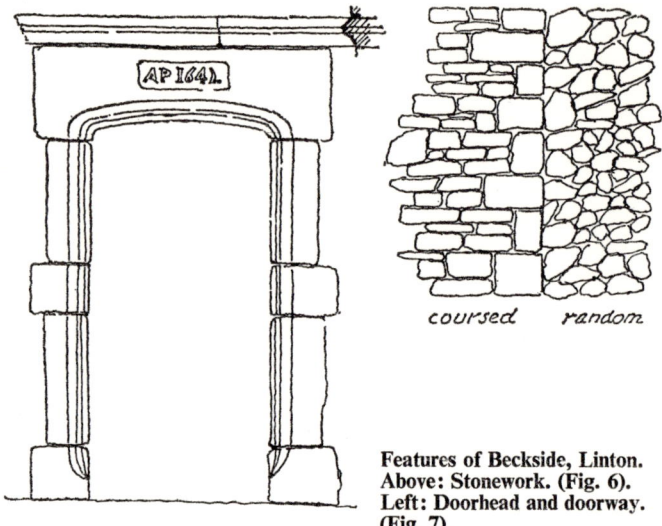

coursed   random

Features of Beckside, Linton.
Above: Stonework. (Fig. 6).
Left: Doorhead and doorway.
(Fig. 7).

are later additions. Facing this old house is a cottage converted from a farm building—note the stone archway now filled in. At one time the room above was a "Reading Room" for the villagers; this cottage had an extension built on about 1938. The two garages are the latest buildings in this "fold," and are very much in keeping with the older structures.

Turning south and to the right along the road, the next cottage is another, rather smaller seventeenth century building with much altered windows. The next one was also built in the seventeenth century and has undergone much quite good alteration of windows; it is traditionally the birth place of Richard Fountaine. The last house along the road was for long known as "Sheepshanks" after a family who occupied it in the eighteenth and early nineteenth centuries. The present building is largely "Georgian," obviously influenced by the almshouses. On the half landing of the centrally-placed hall and stairway is a so-called "Venetian" window copied from the chapel window of the almshouse; it is seen on the north wall of the house. At the front of the house are "Georgian" sash windows of three lights—one wide, two narrow. Let into the thickness of the wall at their sides are shallow cupboards which contained the folding shutters that covered the windows at night. This building which looks so typically Georgian stands on an earlier foundation, shown by the mullioned window (a recent replacement of an older one) on the west wall, a part of the house that is narrower than the rest. This house also has another unusual feature—a stone-vaulted cellar. Looking at the house from the front, we notice a massive stone wall with rectangular openings which are something like cupboards without doors. These are "bee-boles" in which the old fashioned straw bee-skeps were placed for the winter, well sheltered from the cold north and east winds.

Returning along the road to the top of the steps from the footbridge, we turn to the right up a rather narrow lane. At the left-hand corner is an interesting cottage with a good doorway. The stone jambs are moulded and the headstone over it bears a crossed "I" followed by the letters "T" and "A." The "T" gives the surname Topham, the crossed "I" is really a "J" and stands for John, and the "A" is for Alice. Round the corner is a small window with a semi-circular head, and a larger mullioned window. The side of the cottage that looks over the green has an interesting mullioned window with three lights of which the central one is taller—this shape of window occurs fairly frequently in Dales cottages. Facing the building in the lane are two small cottages, built in 1851 and now made into one. They were obviously erected to house the increasing number of textile workers coming to live in the village and work at the mill down by the river, and they show just what kind of buildings were put up for the "labouring classes" when there were no building bye-laws. These were squeezed into an odd piece of land almost touching the house next to them. They face north and get the minimum of sunlight and had the minimum of accommodation—a living-kitchen and a scullery from which rose the staircase. Above was one bedroom and a large landing! This was a perfectly common type of the mid-nineteenth century and can be found in many villages. Today, these buildings have usually been improved by throwing two cottages into one, and by enclosing the landing to make a second small bedroom.

Further up this lane, which is a cul-de-sac, there are three houses, all of them being rebuilt barns. The first one, on the left, was a complete pulling-down and rebuilding, using the old stone for the walls. It was moved back from the road to give a garden in front as well as in the rear, and shows how a modern house can be built in complete harmony with the older parts of the village. In the other two, the barns retain their original walls, roofs and roof timbers, so that the alterations, apart from windows, are entirely internal to make the necessary divisions into two storeys and various rooms. The result shows houses conforming very closely to the traditional pattern. Like most of the seventeenth century houses in this area, the main rooms all face south to get the maximum of sun, heat and light. Returning down the lane to the road and turning right, we pass a cottage adjoining the Topham cottage. It has a much altered frontage, though the back shows remains of altered mullioned windows.

Beyond this, separated by a narrow lane, is the youth hostel. This was formerly the rectory of Linton parish, but was sold about 1930 so that the rector could live in Grassington, the largest village of the parish. In the right-hand corner of the garden are still a few scattered stones indicating the site of the former rectory of the second mediety. After the two medieties were united, the second rectory was used as a farmhouse for the glebe-land, but was allowed to fall into decay and was finally pulled down in the late nineteenth century as the population continued to fall. The youth hostel shows in its windows the various changes since its first building as a rectory in the seventeenth century. There is still one mullioned window on the ground floor at the back. In the eighteenth century, the building was extended by adding a room on each floor at the east end, while sash windows replaced the mullioned windows along the whole front. In the 1890s single-pane sashes replaced the Georgian many-paned windows, leaving just one of these at the west end. The bay-window was added at this time, while the last extension was a large bed-sitting room and bathroom built on to the rear of the house. The garden has a fine show of snowdrops and daffodils in the spring.

Beyond the old rectory, there is another conversion of barn into house, just completed and making along with the two adjacent houses a very attractive corner of Linton. Next to this before crossing the road, is the old Manor House, now divided into two cottages. It has an enclosed garden in which is a group of five old yew trees. Permission to plant these was given by James I, in order to provide wood for long bows—for the people to practise archery! Yews could only be planted in enclosed gardens as the leaves and berries are poisonous to domestic animals; this is the reason for their being so largely confined to graveyards which have always been totally enclosed. The Manor House shows how it has been altered, the clearest signs being on the eastern gable. There is the trace of a mullioned window, altered when all the windows on the main frontage were made into Georgian sashes. It is also possible by examining the stonework to see that the front and back walls have been raised, and the roof-line flattened so that the timbers could sustain the weight of the new stone-slated roof which replaced the earlier thatched roof. There are also remains of earlier windows on the north wall.

Across the main road, the present post-office also shows eighteenth century alterations. The actual windows are new, but they replace old "Georgian type" ones with great fidelity. The plan of the building is typical seventeenth century. Beyond this cottage up another short lane is the last of the old houses of Linton. Now called "White Abbey" in the completely mistaken idea that it was once a grange of Fountains Abbey, it was formerly known as Troutbeck and was a farmhouse. The frontage shows how windows and doorways have undergone considerable changes since its first erection as a typical "yeoman's house." The big extensions at the back are late nineteenth century. This house was for over twenty years the home of Halliwell Sutcliffe, the Yorkshire novelist, whose novels dealt almost exclusively with the Craven district.

The charm of Linton lies in its green and its beck, and the houses of many dates all fitting in with each other because of similar building materials and roof-lines, even though the windows may be of different centuries. One feature is of especial interest. All the old buildings that can be definitely dated as seventeenth century face to the south, or at most a few degrees east or west of true south. They may face the road (Old Hall, White Abbey, Post Office), turn their backs com-

pletely to the road (Manor House, Home Croft) or their gable
ends to the road (Beckside, the Cottage, Brows View, the
Grange). It was more important to get the maximum sun's heat
and light than to face one's neighbours. In the eighteenth
century, houses might face anyway including due north, as in
the case of four of the almshouses. This was an idea imported
from Italy with Renaissance building traditions, for there
shelter *from* sunlight and heat was more important than
exposure *to* it! A detailed study of any one of the old seventeenth century houses shows that the builders had plenty of
common sense in choosing their sites (near to water, sheltered
by hills) and deciding the aspect (south-east, south or south-
west) of the house. They put few windows and fewer doors on
the north side—only staircase and pantry—but every living
room and bedroom faced the sun. The mullioned windows,
with their deeply splayed sides and tops and their window seats
below, let in a surprising amount of light without exposing too
large a glass surface for the dissipation of heat. The thick stone
walls, often two feet or more, and the thick stone-slates of the
roof all helped to conserve heat in the house—very important
when fuel was scarce.

A Walk Round Threshfield

From Grassington Square to Threshfield it is best to go by
car. Old Threshfield begins where the road from Burnsall
converges on the Skipton road. Turning left at this point we
soon reach the "Park" (Fig. 9), all that is left of the old
village green and now enclosed to prevent it becoming merely
a car park. From this point, practically all the old village is
within sight or within reach by very short walks. Across the
main road is the *Old Hall Inn*, formerly the *New Inn*, a late
eighteenth century building with nineteenth century windows
replacing the Georgian sash windows at the front. At the back
the original Georgian windows with their small panes remain in
place. Behind the inn there are a number of old farm buildings,
possibly of sixteenth century date and a part of a much older
building, the real Old Hall. It has on the east side a long
mullioned window of six lights, each having a semi-circular
head and carved spandrells. There is a similar four-light window

on the north side. These windows are identical with those in the remaining portion of the original monastic grange at Kilnsey. This Old Hall is probably the oldest existing domestic building in Upper Wharfedale, older even than the oldest part of Grassington Old Hall and possibly early fourteenth century.

One of the cottages facing the green has a doorhead on which "W 1625 H" is carved, suggesting that it was built by a member of the Hewitt family (p. 23). Turning round with these buildings on our right, we face a row of small cottages separated by a short cul-de-sac from another two small cottages which adjoin a striking example of seventeenth century building on the extreme right. This is now called Park Grange, a modern name, but it has its date and the initials of its builder on the stone over the door head, "F 1640 H." It belonged to Francis Hewitt, another member of the same large family and is built of well-squared masonry with fine mullioned windows, the whole building showing no signs of weathering.

Going up the cul-de-sac, we pass first on the left a house dated 1905 but built in the old style and on an old site by the late Sir Matthew W. Wilson. The extreme left-hand part is a bit of the original building and has a seventeenth century doorway. On the right-hand of the road is a much larger building, Toft House, with a very broad gable on the road side showing it to be two rooms deep. The original mullioned windows have been replaced by modern ones on the front of the building, but not at the back of the house, though some have been extended upwards to give more light to the ground floor rooms. Returning to the Park, we pass a row of much-altered cottages and another house with sash windows at the front but mullions at the back. Continuing towards the bridge, we next see on the left a well-built house with tall Victorian sash windows, but we get a real surprise when we see in the gable end its lovely porch with a continuous mullioned window on the first floor and a beautiful rose window above, possibly Tudor in date as it is Tudor in style. A careful look at the walling on this gable shows traces of jambs of earlier windows, possibly mullioned ones that were built up when new openings were made to accommodate the sash windows.

Beyond this house (the Manor House) is a very fine large shippon with three well-made doorways in the gable, each having triangular spandrells in the door-head. One has the date, 1661, on its headstone; another the initials M.H. (for Matthew Hewitt) and the third is left plain. The middle door leads to the "fother gang," the paved way between a row of "boosts" for cattle on either side and a common feature of the larger "shippons" in the dales. The next house has also had its windows altered, but one old small window suggests that it was probably built in the seventeenth century. The outbuilding in its backyard has an outside staircase leading into a room with a fireplace. Such a minimum dwelling was often the home of a farm servant (a hind) and was very handy for keeping an eye on the cattle below!

Across the road is another interesting house, showing successive stages of "improving" and "modernising." The back has one mullioned window and traces of others, and an old doorway with an arched headstone. This house was extended in the eighteenth century with a symmetrical frontage and sash windows with the small Georgian panes of glass. Recently these have been replaced by modern casements and a small porch added to the front. This hides the old doorhead marking the Georgian alterations with its lettering "C D 1771."

The road continues over the bridge, crossing Threshfield Beck with the old ford alongside. One cannot help noticing the enormous stones used to "top" the parapets and shaped into a semicircular form with deeply cut longitudinal grooves. They are six or more feet long; similar stones are found on several of the old bridges in this neighbourhood and probably came from the old quarries on Thorpe Fell. On the far side of the stream is Ling Hall, rebuilt after a disastrous fire so that no old features remain except the numerous shoes—horse shoes, pony shoes and cow shoes fixed on the barn door in the correct position so that the good luck they bring will not run out! This house was for a long time occupied by the Ibbotson family. The best known member was "Besom Jamie," who made besoms or brooms from heather twigs or birch twigs. The "engine" that he used to grip and tighten the bundles of twigs is now in the Craven Museum in Skipton.